Lake Superior

ST. IGNACE

Lake Huron

St. Lawrence River

Fox River

WISCONSIN PORTAGE

GREEN BAY

Mississippi River

Wisconsin River

Lake Michigan

KASKASKIA INDIAN VILLAGE

CHICAGO PORTAGE

ILLINOIS INDIAN VILLAGE

Illinois River

Missouri River

Ohio River

ARKANSAS INDIAN VILLAGE

Mississippi River

Cornerstones of Freedom

The Story of
MARQUETTE
AND
JOLLIET

By R. Conrad Stein

Illustrated by Richard Wahl

 CHILDRENS PRESS, CHICAGO

Library of Congress Cataloging in Publication Data

Stein, R. Conrad.
  The story of Marquette and Jolliet.

  (Cornerstones of freedom)
  Summary: Describes the seventeenth-century expedition
undertaken by two Frenchman, a priest and a soldier,
that led to the European discovery of the upper
Mississippi.
  1.   Mississippi River—Discovery and exploration—
Juvenile literature.   2.   Joliet, Louis, 1645-1700—
Juvenile literature.   3.   Marquette, Jacques, 1637-1675—
Juvenile literature.   4.   Explorers—America—Biography—
Juvenile literature.   5.   Explorers—France—Biography—
Juvenile literature. |1.   Mississippi River—Discovery
and exploration.   2.   Joliet, Louis, 1645-1700.
3.   Marquette, Jacques, 1637-1675.   4.   Explorers|
I.   Wahl, Richard, 1939-   II.   Title.   III.   Series.
F352.S 83   977'.01   81-5036
ISBN 0-516-04630-6   AACR2

  6 7 8 9 10 R 90 89

Seven Frenchmen in two canoes paddled over the calm waters of Lake Michigan. They were leaving the mission church at St. Ignace, where Lake Michigan and Lake Huron come together. That church was one of the most distant French settlements in the New World.

These seven men were explorers. They were heading for land no European had ever seen before. Leading the expedition were Louis Jolliet and Father Jacques Marquette. It was mid-May, 1673.

Marquette and Jolliet followed a course they had planned months earlier. They sailed south on Lake Michigan to the finger of water now called Green Bay. The canoes hugged the shore as they glided through the water.

The travelers saw a wild and beautiful forest land. Pine-covered cliffs jutted out of the blue waters. Deer leaped about in the clearings. Bears, wolves, and foxes roamed the woods. Beavers and playful otters splashed in the sparkling streams that emptied into the bay.

A tribe of Indians called the Menominees lived near Green Bay. They were friends of the French. These Indians lived mainly on the delicious wild rice that grows in the area. So the French called them Wild Rice Indians.

Marquette and Jolliet told the Indians they intended to travel west toward "Big Water." The Menominees were horrified. They warned the Frenchmen that to the west the sun burned so hot it could roast a man. And living in the rivers of the west were huge monsters that could swallow a canoe in one gulp. The French knew the Menominees loved to tell tall tales. So they thanked the Indians for the advice, but continued on their way.

Beyond Green Bay, the explorers paddled up the Fox River. Then, with the help of Indian guides, they carried their canoes overland to another river now called the Wisconsin. This river flowed in a new direction—west.

Until now, the waterways the French had explored flowed east. These rivers joined the St. Lawrence River, went past their own cities of Montreal and Quebec, and emptied into the Atlantic Ocean. But the Wisconsin River flowed in the opposite direction. "Thus," said the journal of the expedition, "we left the waters flowing to Quebec to float on those that would thenceforward take us through a strange land."

In a clearing, Father Marquette, a Catholic priest, set up an altar and held Mass. The men dropped to their knees and bowed their heads. They prayed before they plunged into the unknown.

The purpose of the expedition was to explore and claim new land for France. At the time the only

French land in the New World was made up of a few settlements on the St. Lawrence River. This was called New France. Today this area is the province of Quebec in Canada.

The early settlers of New France were fishermen. They became friendly with the Indians of the area. The French admired the furs worn by the Indians. The Frenchmen traded knives and fishhooks for beaver pelts. They took the pelts back to France. Beaver furs were very valuable there. The French quickly discovered they could earn more money by trading for beaver furs than they could by fishing.

Soon more fur traders came to New France. They built some settlements. Two of these later became the great Canadian cities of Montreal and Quebec.

But the settlements grew slowly. Fur traders had to go into the wilderness to get furs. They could not stay for long in the settlements. The companies that traded furs did not help the settlements grow. Fur traders were interested in profits, not in building up cities. Also, Indians often attacked settlers. This discouraged Europeans from coming to New France.

In the mid-1600s, King Louis XIV of France sent a man named Jean Talon to New France. At this time England and Spain were busy carving up the New World. They were trying to claim more and more territory as their own. The king of France told

Talon to expand the territory of New France. He also wanted Talon to make the existing settlements more stable.

Talon studied the reports made by Indians about the land to the west. Frenchmen in canoes had already explored the Great Lakes. Indians claimed that below the Great Lakes there flowed a huge, mysterious river. The river cut through hundreds of miles of land, then emptied into a vast sea. Some Indian tribes called this river "Great Water." Others called it "Father of Waters," or in their language, *Messipi*.

Did this river really exist? Talon wondered. If it did, into which sea did it flow? Since the discovery of America, European sailors had been trying to find a water passage through the huge continent. They wanted to be able to sail directly to Asia. Could this "Great Water" be the gateway to the Orient?

Talon thought of sending a group of men to find the river and see where it led. They could then claim all new-found lands for the king of France. The governor of New France agreed. Talon suggested Jolliet and Marquette as leaders of the expedition. Two better men could not have been found.

The governor appointed Louis Jolliet to be mili-

tary leader of the group. Jolliet was born near
Quebec in New France in 1645. He was the first
explorer of America who was actually born in
America. Jolliet grew up in the rugged Canadian
woodlands. He learned how to hunt and fish while
still a child. He had what every good leader must
have—courage. Father Claude Dablon had once
been Jolliet's teacher. Dablon later wrote of his student, "He had the courage to fear nothing where all
else is feared."

The religious leader of the expedition was Father
Jacques Marquette. He was born to a wealthy

family in France in 1637. He joined the Jesuit order of Catholic priests. In 1666 he came to New France. There, the Jesuits lived with the Indians in hopes of converting the Indians to Christianity. Marquette went through bitter winters in Indian villages with a smile. He slept in freezing huts and often went without food. He cared more about winning new souls for Christ than he cared about food or a warm place to sleep.

Marquette was also a great scholar, and learned to speak six different Indian languages. His knowledge of these languages would be very important during the expedition with Jolliet.

It took the expedition a week to paddle about one hundred miles down the Wisconsin River. On June 17, 1673, they reached a point where the Wisconsin joined a broad, gently flowing river that ran south. Marquette, Jolliet, and their party became the first Europeans to see the upper Mississippi River.

They had made their first goal. The Frenchmen had reached "Big Water." Now their task was to follow the river to its mouth. Would it lead them west to the Pacific Ocean?

Steadily the expedition paddled south. Along the way they caught fish for their meals. To do this they just dropped nets over the sides of their canoes. In those days the upper Mississippi was a fisherman's dream. The Frenchmen wrote that the water ran so clear they could see "pike and catfish up to 150 pounds, redhorse and perch that ranged between three and ten feet." One of these monster fish, Marquette wrote, "struck so violently against our canoe that I took it for a large tree about to knock us to pieces."

Both riverbanks were alive with animals. The explorers saw deer and huge moose calmly drinking water. Having rarely seen people before, the animals had no fear of human beings. They looked at the canoes curiously. Then they returned to their drinking. On one morning the voyagers saw a mountain lion or a lynx swimming across the river. They described it as "a monster with the head of a tiger, a pointed snout like a wild-cat's, a beard and ears erect, a grayish head and neck all black."

The explorers had seen no Indians since leaving Green Bay.

Jolliet, the military leader, had mixed feelings about meeting any Indians. He hoped to meet a friendly tribe who could tell him something about the land farther down the river. But he feared a meeting with the Indians called the Iroquois. The five tribes of the Iroquois nation lived in the north-eastern section of what is now the United States. They were fierce and often cruel fighters. They hated the French and any Indian tribes friendly with the French.

As the seven men paddled down the river, Jolliet's eyes looked left and right. He kept a watch on both banks of the river. His tiny group would have no chance in a fight with the Iroquois.

Marquette, the religious leader, looked forward to meeting Indians. He wanted to try to convert them to Christianity. And no wilderness priest was ever more devoted to his duty than Jacques Marquette. That devotion made him as fearless as the bravest French soldier.

Near what is today the city of Quincy, Illinois the explorers caught sight of a trail. It led from the riverbank into the forest. In the mud they saw fresh footprints. Jolliet and Marquette left their five companions to guard the canoes. They followed the trail. Soon they came to an Indian village. Not wanting to sneak up on the village, Jolliet stepped into a clearing. He cupped his hands around his mouth and yelled, "Hello!" Then he held his breath, hoping the Indians were not hostile.

The Indians of the village froze in their tracks. Then they turned to face Jolliet. At first they cried out to each other while pointing wildly at the Frenchman. Finally, four men approached. In the middle of the group was a wrinkled, white-haired man. He held a peace pipe. Clearly, these Indians wished to talk and be friends.

The four were chiefs of a tribe called the Illinois. Only a few of them had ever seen a white man before. The Illinois hoped the Frenchmen could help them protect themselves from the Iroquois. The tribe had often been raided by Iroquois war parties. They had been forced to move their village many times.

The chiefs were also very pleased to meet the Jesuit priest Marquette. The Indians of the north called Jesuits "Black Robes" because the priests wore black vestments. The Black Robes were known to be gentle, kind, and willing to share anything they had with Indians. Even the faraway Illinois tribe knew of them.

Marquette and Jolliet sat with the four Illinois chiefs and smoked the peace pipe. The Illinois language was similar to Algonkian. Marquette knew Algonkian, so he talked to the Illinois. He soon won their trust.

Before the Frenchmen left the village, the old chief invited them to a feast. The Frenchmen agreed. They soon would learn the Illinois tribe had customs very different from their own!

After the chief delivered a long speech, a dinner was served. It was a stew made from roast buffalo

hump and boiled dog. Worse yet, the ancient chief took pieces of the stew out of the bowl with his fingers and put them directly into the Frenchmen's mouths! This was the way the Illinois tribe treated guests of honor.

When the two Frenchmen finally left, Marquette promised the Illinois he would return. The old chief presented the priest with a peace pipe. Neither Marquette nor Jolliet knew how important that peace pipe would become.

As they continued down the river, the explorers discovered the "monsters" the Wild Rice Indians had warned them about. On the flat side of a cliff, the journal states, they "saw two monsters painted on one of these rocks, which startled us at first." Towering above them were weird rock drawings of two figures. The figures looked like men, but had "horns on the head like a deer, a terrifying look, red eyes." The pictures were not merely scribbled on the rock. The journal goes on to say, "Good painters in France would find it hard to do as well."

Other explorers later found more of these cliff drawings. Even early settlers farming in Illinois and Missouri saw these eerie rock paintings and wrote about them. The paintings were the work of local Indians. No one knows why the Indians painted such strange figures. Today the pictures are gone. Centuries of rain have washed them away.

In late June, the expedition paddled into another surprise. Marquette wrote, "Sailing quietly in clear, calm water, we heard the noise of a rapid, into which we were about to run." To his right a huge river gushed out of the forest and thundered into the Mississippi. Its waters flowed chocolate brown. Giant uprooted trees spun madly in the water.

Luckily, the Frenchmen were expert canoeists and had gone through, or shot, rapids before. Still, it took all their skills to paddle safely through this rushing water.

The Marquette and Jolliet expedition had come to the spot where the Missouri River joins the Mississippi. This is where St. Louis stands today. The huge Missouri flows from the west. The explorers saw it when the river was swollen with melting snow from the far-off Rocky Mountains. The mighty Missouri had picked up whole trees, boulders, and anything else in its path. It sent this mess tumbling into the Mississippi. The gush of water was so powerful that it made the earth tremble. About this joining of two great rivers Marquette wrote, "I have seen nothing more dreadful."

As the party went farther south, the countryside grew more tropical. Gradually, cottonwood and elm trees grew in place of pines. Bright-colored birds darted over the water. The Frenchmen described one kind as "a little parrot with half the head red, the rest, with the neck, yellow, and the body green." It was probably a Carolina parakeet. This species, once common in the southern marshlands, became extinct in the early 1900s.

While rounding a bend in the present state of Arkansas, the party came to an Indian village. Jolliet ordered his men to paddle toward it. He hoped the Indians would be peaceful. Suddenly a dozen dugout canoes, each carrying three or four Indians, splashed toward the Frenchmen. On the riverbank, braves—screaming war cries—appeared out of the woods. They were armed with tomahawks and bows and arrows. Several braves dove into the water and swam toward the two French canoes. Other Indians fired arrows and threw tomahawks from the shore.

Jolliet, thinking quickly, remembered the peace pipe the Illinois chief had given them. Even though arrows were whistling over his head, Jolliet stood straight up in his canoe. He raised the peace pipe above him. Meanwhile, Marquette used every language he knew to yell to the braves that the party had come in peace. Finally a chief on the river-bank saw the peace pipe. He ordered his men to stop the attack.

Marquette bowed his head. He thanked God that this battle had ended so quickly.

On the riverbank, the Frenchmen sat with the Indians and smoked the peace pipe. These Indians were members of the Quapaw tribe. Attacks by out-siders had made the Quapaw wary of strangers, but they still honored the peace pipe. The Quapaws did not speak a language that Marquette knew. So the priest had to use sign language. The Quapaws told him their village was about a ten-day journey from a huge sea. Sailing on that sea were other white men in tall ships.

Jolliet listened and nodded. He knew Spanish forces were in the southern part of the continent. The men in the tall ships had to be Spaniards. Since the Spanish and the French were enemies, Jolliet decided to go back north. He did not want to risk leading the party "into the hands of the Spanish, who without a doubt would at least have detained us as captives."

The members of the expedition turned their canoes around. They started upstream for home. They had not reached the mouth of the Mississippi, but they now knew where the river ran. It flowed south and emptied into the Gulf of Mexico. Jolliet would report that the Mississippi was not the gateway to the Orient. The great river was vital to New France, however, because it was a passage to Mexico.

Now paddling against the current, the Frenchmen slowly pushed their canoes north. Near the mouth of the Ohio River, they again met some members of the Illinois tribe. The Indians advised the explorers to take a shortcut to Lake Michigan. They said to go up a river that is now called the Illinois. The Illinois would lead to a marshland the French could walk across to get to the lake. The Indians called this marsh *Checagou.*

Jolliet decided to take the Indians' advice. The Frenchmen paddled northeast up the Illinois River. That river led to a branch later called the Des Plaines. Soon the explorers found the marshland. They carried their canoes across it to a large stream that emptied into Lake Michigan. Later Jolliet wrote in a letter that this marshland should someday

be the site of a settlement, or perhaps even a major city. A canal dug here would connect Lake Michigan to the Mississippi. That inland waterway would allow ships to sail from the North Atlantic to the Gulf of Mexico.

In 1848 that canal was completed. Today, the great city of Chicago spreads over the ground where Marquette and Jolliet once carried their canoes.

At Lake Michigan, the explorers paddled three hundred miles up the coast to a tiny Jesuit mission near Green Bay. They spent the winter there. In the spring Marquette and Jolliet parted. Jolliet headed toward Montreal. Marquette decided to return to the Illinois tribe to continue his missionary work. The two friends shook hands and went separate ways. They had no idea they would never see each other again.

It was a smooth trip for Jolliet over the Great Lakes and through the St. Lawrence River. Near Montreal he faced the dangerous Lachine Rapids. Jolliet had two choices. He could carry his canoe overland around the rapids, or he could try to shoot them. Jolliet decided to shoot the rapids because that was the fastest way. He was in a hurry to get home.

In the middle of the Lachine Rapids his canoe spun out of control. The craft slammed sideways into a rock and broke into pieces. The current pulled Jolliet under the water. He hit his head on a boulder and was knocked out. His unconscious body was finally pulled out of the river by some men who had been fishing on the bank. The strongbox containing maps and notes Jolliet had made during the journey lay somewhere on the bottom of the St. Lawrence River—forever lost to history.

Jolliet had commanded an expedition that took his party through more than 2,500 miles of unknown land. Now, just a few miles from home, he had made his only bad decision—to shoot the Lachine Rapids.

When Jolliet finally recovered from his near-drowning in the rapids, he continued on to Montreal. There he discovered that his sponsor, Jean Talon, had gone to France. Jolliet had no one to report to. His maps and notes were at the bottom of the river. Jolliet felt the entire voyage had been wasted.

Jolliet made more explorations for New France in the next decades. For his services to the government he was given an island in the Gulf of St. Lawrence. He also was honored with titles from the French king. Jolliet died in 1700.

Father Jacques Marquette carried on his missionary work after parting from Jolliet. At Green Bay the priest became ill. This kept him from returning to the Illinois village until mid-November, 1674. In

the Great Lakes region, November is not a good
time to begin a journey. A winter storm halted Marquette and his small party at the marshland at the
tip of Lake Michigan. Marquette built a hut from
mud and logs. The missionary settled there for the
winter. That hut was located on the south side of
what is today the city of Chicago.

Then, as now, Chicago winters were brutal. Marquette and his party might have starved. But the
black-robed priest was so loved by the Indians that
local tribes brought food to him.

In the spring of 1675 Marquette reached the
Illinois village. The people greeted him as a long-lost

friend. He preached for a few weeks, but became ill
again. This time the priest felt his death was near.
He asked his party to take him to the mission church
at St. Ignace, where the Marquette and Jolliet
expedition had begun.

They started toward St. Ignace, but Father Marquette was too weak for the voyage. He died on the
shores of Lake Michigan. He was buried near the
mouth of what is now the Marquette River in
Michigan. His party claimed the priest died with his
eyes looking at heaven and a smile on his face. He
was thirty-eight years old.

Two years later, in thirty canoes, Indians who had recently become Christians came ashore at the spot where Marquette was buried. They took the priest's body from the ground and carried it north to the mission at St. Ignace. There they gave Father Marquette a proper Christian funeral, as they knew he would have wished.

For many years afterward, the Marquette and Jolliet expedition was hardly mentioned in books about North America. But today we know that the two courageous Frenchmen were the European discoverers of the upper Mississippi.

About the Author:

Mr. Stein was born and grew up in Chicago. He attended the University of Illinois and graduated with a degree in history. He later studied in Mexico and earned a more advanced degree from the University of Guanajuato.

While a student, Mr. Stein worked during the summers as a sailor on iron-ore carrying ships in the Great Lakes. From the decks of those ships he has often been overwhelmed by the beauty of the forest land stretching along the shores. In some areas this rugged land looks much the same now as it did to the explorers of New France three hundred years ago.

About the Artist:

Richard Wahl, graduate of the Art Center College of Design in Los Angeles, has illustrated a number of magazine articles and booklets. He is a skilled artist and photographer who advocates realistic interpretations of his subjects. He lives with his wife and two sons in Louisville, Kentucky.